If My Body Could Sing

The Rhythm in my Heart.

By

Erica, Porter

Table of Contents

POEM I: Knock. Knock.. Knock…

POEM II: Let The World Remember Us.

POEM III: Together, And Ever With You.

POEM IV: Tasty In Deep Ocean.

POEM V: And So Has Everything Suddenly Changed.

POEM VI: Darkest Moments.

POEM VII: Old Time Religion.

POEM VIII: Trapped In Life.

POEM IV: Being Original Is Key.

POEM X: Ugly Company.

POEM XI: Light On.

Poem I

Knock. Knock. Knock…

****

#1

Knocking at your door,
You didn't answer my call,
I didn't have the strength to roar,

No time to waste any further,
No time to lose,
I had to leave.

You needed me to come,
It wasn't yet time to die,
The footpath across your stairwells,

#2

We had issues reciprocating,
I like to prolong issues,
You weren't open to me,

My footprints are hunting,
I had to exit the door,
Straight into your life,

The nightmares are back again,
The emptiness is huge,
The horror lives inside of you,
You scare me,

#3

We can walk in or work out,
Anyway, we choose,
Maybe we can figure them out or not,

However we do,
We can't live without,
We can't live to lose,

The heavy knock,
I thought it was us,
My heart aches once more,

Poem II

Let The World Remember Us

****

#1

Let's take this shot,
Paste it on the wall,
Just so you always remember,

Print multiple copies of us,
Throw them into the blue skies,
Let the sun show a reflection of us,

We were here,
Always,
And steal,

#2

Flash it on the ground,
Find what's hidden beneath,
And if we eventually do,

Though we don't ever want to,
The clenched teeth,
And the sleeping eyes,

Never wanted to go,
But we have to someday,
So let the world know,

#3

Paint a cupful of ink,
With my ever-warm lips,
Brush off the blushes,

Print a sexy kiss,
On your stainless laps,
Off your beautiful face,

Maybe we could mold our status,
Hurt the hearts that loved us,
We could inflict some pain,

Poem III

Together, And Ever With You

****

#1

We become all we wanna be,
Only if we try,
Our reincarnated souls,
Who truly believes,

Eternity is for us,
Hopefully, we shall die one day,
We all know about it,
Whoever ran away from it,

Call it homecoming,
Call it a reunion,
Even the last supper,
Maybe they are all fairytales,

#2

Where does the soul go,
After its parting from the flesh,
How well do you believe,

If you never lived it right,
Nor make things bigger,
You're never eager,
You know it's better,

Be you a wealthy philanthropist,
Elevate your souls to demons,
But as wretched witchcraft,
You've turned to carnivorous,

#3

Disconcerting experience is life,
The world is in a topsy-turvy state,
The dark moon,
And the frowning sun,

The invincible covers,
You always hide in,
The dark spot In your heart,
Kills everyone who stares,

Pa is the best company,
Resentment defeats friendship,
Not even your nagging Ma,
I might not want to share,

Poem IV

Tasty In Deep Ocean

****

#1

Serve me a glass of wine,
I need a saving Grace,
Letting off this mess,
We only live to try,

Acceptance was all you prayed for,
But I gave my love and care,
We still might not be all that is to life,
They promised us Heaven,
When all they needed was Earth,

What about the life He gave,
When I could neither breathe,
I gave you health and wealth,
Though I couldn't earn a living,

#2

Never won a single game,
Losing is neither an option,
We try or not,
What difference does it make,

Try all we could,
Failure is all you get,
Stumbling and falling,
The rhythm of the brave,

There's no climbing up the stairs,
How do we make it big,
By not losing hope,

#3

Not looking down to the ground,
There is no cuddle,
I never saw a coward,

Stumbling and falling,
The tool of the handicapped,
It molds life into us,

Falling and rising,
We race off to greatness,
We never lose hopelessness,

Poem V

And So Has Everything Suddenly Changed

****

#1

My prayers, The answers,
My requests, Their negligence,
My endeavors, Their outcome,
My beliefs, Their disbelieve,

My perfections, Their imperfections,
My existence, Their critiques,
My actions, Their reactions,
My stillness, Their utterances,

My squabbles, their travesty,
My embrace, their defiance,
My declaration, their contradictions,
My affection, their resentment,

The city of Sodom
And that of Babylon,
No Much Difference,

Poem VI

Darkest Moments

****

#1

Why are those Rumpled complexions,
It's hurting bad,
I speak to you about it,
But all we heard were silent voices,

You have something to say,
I can see it in your eyes,
The Shutter's mouth,
They won't let you say a word,

Your Muted lips are sealed,
Like the letter from my mama,
I've been in this cold cell,
Fighting the demons in me,

#2

My little small hole,
The darkest part of life,
Our entanglement with fear,
To unknowing affairs,

I shut ‘em all out,
Hope you understand,
What it's like to be demons,

I feel left out and alone,
It's hurting me inside,
Fighting my inner peace to hate you,
Don't wish you what I pass through,

Poem VII

Old Time Religion

****

#1

Where are you?
Where have you gone?
Our roundtable gathering.

What happened to love and care?
Our hearts are so hard and dark,
So wounded and dripping wet.

The eyes of men far from our hearts,
What happened to the days of fervent prayers,
Thoughtful moments of the midnight tears,

#2

Fierce words from a caring Dad?
Exhorting smiles of a caring Mom,
The sounds of flying strokes replaced the solemn tremor of concern,

The dedicatory prayers during the morning and bedtime devotions are gone,
All I hear now are the dreadful sounds of a beating drum (like on the parade ground),
Mom stopped sobbing and started whipping,
Dad stopped talking but started drinking.

The drum surfaces are so wounded now.
The drumsticks are all broken.
The canes as a tool for punishment, replaced the eyes being the organs of watchful and passionate upbringing,

Where are those words of their hearts?
Where is the love of our parents??
Bring back the old methods to us.
We're crying and sobering.

Poem VIII

Trapped In Life

****

#1

Mesmerize me with your beauty,
Win me over like a game,
I can't resist all that you bring,
I'm Compromised,

If all that's required is my heart;
I've been Sacrificed,
Close the entrance to this paradise,
I'll improvise,

Leave me with a thousand choices,
I take my chances,
Make your heart a bet,
There's no escaping,

#2

Dry dust uprooted,
Dry leaves danced to the ground,
Tree branches wave to their creator,
We await thy dropping tears,

Clouds race to a fate unknown,
Running faster than my eyes,
Try to retrace its steps,
We never going back,

Themyts feasting on the host,
Caskets enclose the cabin man,
The graveyard is our dwelling place,
The world's temporary home,

#3

It's another Saturday in Sidney,
Before Sunday it's usually sunny,
A day at the casino cruise,
She's beautiful and silly,

Just like centuries,
The last time we spoke,
The Caribbean angels,
This feeling is classic,

Poem IV

Being Original Is Key

****

#1

It's a tough decision fighting the demons in you,

But a huge and admirable acceptance to live with them,

In the end; being who you wanna be,

Doing exactly what you wanna do,

No matter how 'Difficult', 'Off', or 'Stupid' it seems,

Poem X

Ugly Company

****

#1

Where we all started,
On the 2nd day of June,
In the reflections on my past,
What do we make of those,

We're here again,
Thinking about our past,
It seems like every summer,
But we're no longer the same,

These shady pieces of life,
I gave all of myself to me,
It left me with nothing new,
I grew right back on track,

I never said no to me,
'caus, I don't believe in it,
They only turned away,
'caus they look so ugly now.

We were meant to bear,
But we choose not to care,
What then are we doing here,
Without each other,

Poem XI

Light On

****

#1

Seated on the armrest of the couch,
Lost in thought,
The world has been evacuated,

Agony evolved into a preferred place for survival,
Drinking so bitter and sad,
Thoughts far away from reality,

Narrowly deflected by the sound of a waging door,
Sent off to the open field for shelter,
Unduly swathed for the occasion,

www.ingramcontent.com/pod-product-compliance
Lightning Source LLC
LaVergne TN
LVHW052109160826
845678LV00015B/3444

* 9 7 9 8 8 4 6 3 6 6 6 2 6 *